Schorndorf

Geburtshaus von Gottlieb Daimler in der Höllgasse 7 mit Daimlers Motorkutsche von 1886

The house in Höllgasse 7, at which Gottlieb Daimler was born, and Daimler's motor coach of 1886

Maison natale de Gottlieb Daimler (Höllgasse 7) et sa « calèche à moteur » de 1886.

Gabriel Habermann

Schorndorf

Text von · Text by · Texte de
Winfried Kübler

Deutsch · English · Français

Silberburg-Verlag

Das Schorndorfer Rathaus wurde 1730 erbaut.

Schorndorf town hall was built in 1730.

La mairie de Schorndorf a été bâtie en 1730.

Hübsche Details vom Balkon und vom Portal des Rathauses

Fine details of the town hall's balcony and portal

Charmants détails du balcon et du portail de la mairie

Im Rathausturm befindet sich ein Glockenspiel, das vom Handels- und Gewerbeverein gestiftet wurde.

The chimes in the tower of the town hall were donated by the Association of Commerce and Industry.

Dans la tour de la mairie se trouve un carillon offert par l'Association des artisans et des commerçants.

Das Palm'sche Wappen auf dem Schlussstein des mittleren Portals

The Palm family's coat of arms on the keystone of the middle portal

Le blason de la famille Palm sur la clef du portail médian

Palm'sche Apotheke: eine Konsole, die als Neidkopf ausgebildet ist

Palm's Apothecary: set into a bracket, a "Neidkopf", which is meant to protect the house-owner from the envy of others.

La pharmacie Palm : console sculptée en forme de tête conjuratoire

Mercedes-Veteranen auf dem Marktplatz

Mercedes vintage cars on the market square

De vieux modèles de Mercedes sur la place du Marché

Das Rathaus, das Café Weiler (einstmals Wohnhaus der Barbara Künkelin) und die Palm'sche Apotheke prägen den Marktplatz der Stadt.

The town hall, Café Weiler (once Barbara Künkelin's home) and Palm's Apothecary are characteristic of the town's market square.

La mairie, le Café Weiler (ancienne habitation de Barbara Künkelin) et la pharmacie Palm, dominent la place du Marché.

Fachwerkdetails und »Neidköpfe« an der Palm'schen Apotheke

Details of half-timbering and "Neidköpfe" on Palm's Apothecary building

Détail d'un colombage et des têtes conjuratoires de la pharmacie Palm

Der gusseiserne Marktbrunnen auf dem Oberen Marktplatz stammt aus dem Jahr 1773 und wurde von den Eisenwerken Königsbronn hergestellt.

The cast-iron fountain on Upper Market Square dates back to 1773 and was produced by the ironworks in Königsbronn.

En haut de la place, la fontaine du marché fabriquée par les fonderies Königsbronn en 1773 est en fonte.

Die Schorndorfer Stadtkirche aus der Vogelschau

Bird's eye view of Schorndorf municipal church

L'église principale de Schorndorf vue du ciel

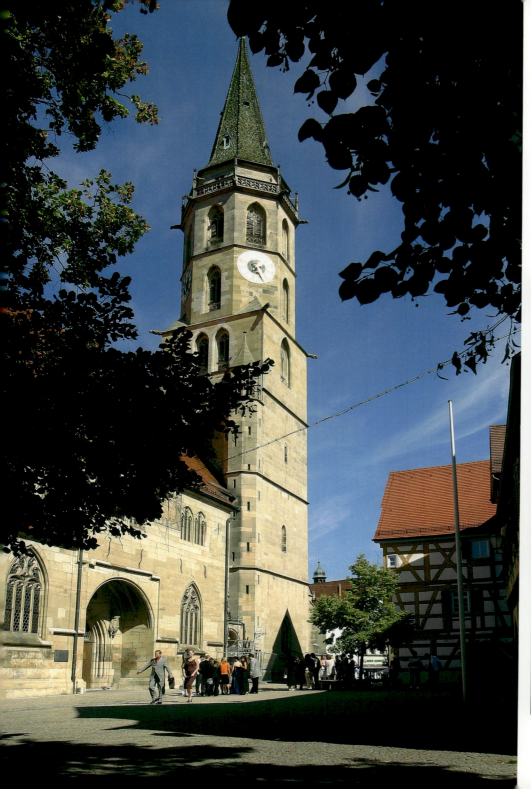

Die gotische Stadtkirche wurde ab dem Jahr 1477 errichtet.

Construction of the Gothic municipal church was started in 1477.

La construction de l'église gothique commença en 1477.

In Karlsruhe wird eine Glocke für die Stadtkirche gegossen.

In Karlsruhe—a bell being cast for the municipal church

La fonderie de Karlsruhe réalise une cloche pour l'église centrale.

Hundsköpfiger Wasserspeier
Gargoyle with the head of a dog
Gargouille à tête de chien

Der heilige Georg, Pfeilerfigur am Chor, und eine Kluge und eine Törichte Jungfrau an der Südfassade (rechts)

Saint George, as a figure on the pillar at the quire, and the "Wise and Foolish Virgins" on the southern façade (right)

Sculpture de Saint Georges sur un pilier du chœur, et une vierge sage et une vierge folle sur la façade sud (à droite)

Der spätgotische Chor der evangelischen Stadtkirche stammt aus dem Jahr 1501.

The Late Gothic quire of the Protestant municipal church dates back to 1501.

Le chœur gothique flamboyant de l'église protestante date de 1501.

Der Chor der Schorndorfer Stadtkirche erstrahlt in hellem Licht.

The quire of Schorndorf municipal church, flooded in bright light

Le chœur de l'église principale de Schorndorf baigne dans la lumière.

Der Stammbaum Jesu als figürliche Wurzel-Jesse-Darstellung findet sich in der Marienkapelle.

Genealogical tree of Jesus in the form of a sculptured root Jesse representation, in the Marienkapelle

La généalogie de Jésus présentée sous forme de racine de Jessé se trouve dans la Marienkapelle.

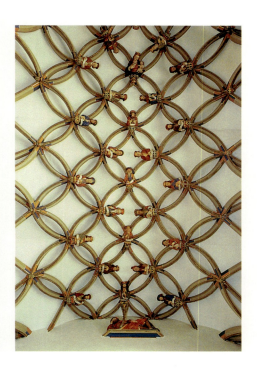

Die katholische Heilig-Geist-Kirche (1955) am Feuersee

The Catholic Church of the Holy Ghost (1955) on the Feuersee

L'église catholique du Saint Esprit (1955) près du Feuersee

Festgottesdienst in der Schorndorfer Heilig-Geist-Kirche

Mass in the Schorndorf Church of the Holy Ghost

L'office lors d'une fête religieuse dans l'église du Saint Esprit

Der Altarraum der Heilig-Geist-Kirche wird vom Pfingstbild des Künstlers Rudolf Kurz beherrscht.

The chancel of the Church of the Holy Ghost is dominated by the Whitsun painting by the artist Rudolf Kurz.

L'imposant tableau de la Pentecôte, de l'artiste Rudolf Kurz, imprègne l'atmosphère autour de l'autel.

Eine Platanenallee führt zum Portal des Alten Friedhofs.

An avenue of plane trees leads to portal of the old cemetery.

Une allée de platanes conduit au portail de l'ancien cimetière.

Im Alten Friedhof findet sich eine hübsche Kapelle.

In the old cemetery there is a lovely chapel .

Dans l'ancien cimetière se trouve une jolie petite chapelle.

Auf dem Adventsmarkt   *Market during the Advent season*   *Marché de Noël*

Beim Weinmarkt in Schorndorf ist der Marktplatz bis auf den letzten Platz gefüllt.

During the wine market Schorndorf's market square is completely and utterly packed.

Pendant la foire aux vins de Schorndorf, la place du Marché est pleine à craquer.

Auch der Wochenmarkt findet auf dem Marktplatz statt.

The weekly market is also held on the market square.

Le marché hebdomadaire se déroule aussi sur la place du Marché.

»SchoWo« (Schorndorfer Woche) heißt das jährliche Stadtfest und ist der Höhepunkt im Festreigen der Stadt.

"SchoWo" (Schorndorf week) is the name of the town's annual festival and represents the climax of the series of festivals that take place there.

Tous les ans, la « SchoWo » (semaine de Schorndorf) marque le point culminant d'une ronde de fêtes.

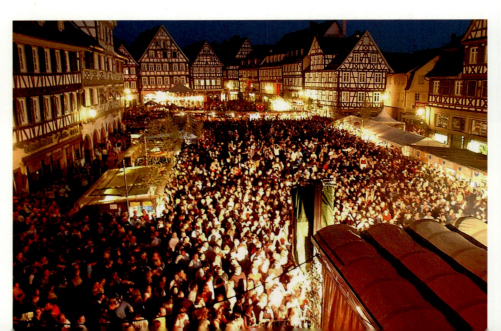

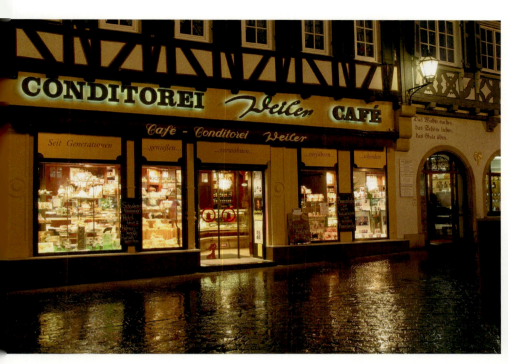

Das ehemalige Wohnhaus der Barbara Künkelin beherbergt heute das Café Weiler.

Barbara Künkelin's former home today accommodates Café Weiler.

L'ancienne habitation de Barbara Künkelin abrite aujourd'hui le Café Weiler.

Im Stadtmuseum am Kirchplatz sind die Geschehnisse um die »Schorndorfer Weiber« bildlich und plastisch dargestellt.

In the town museum on the square Kirchplatz the events relating to the "Women of Schorndorf" are depicted in both paintings and sculptures.

Dans le Musée Municipal, place de l'Eglise, les évènements concernant les « Bonnes Femmes de Schorndorf » sont représentés en peinture et en sculpture.

Die »Schorndorfer Weiber« – das Natursteinmosaik an der Nordfassade des Rathauses stammt von Gottfried von Stockhausen (1965). Es erinnert an den Widerstand der Bürgerinnen und Bürger gegen die Übergabe der Festung Schorndorf an den französischen Feldherrn Mélac im Jahr 1688.

The "Women of Schorndorf"— a mosaic, made of natural stone, on the northern façade of the town hall—was created by Gottfried von Stockhausen (1965). It commemorates the resistance of the town's citizens to the handing over of the fortress Schorndorf to the French general Mélac in the year 1688.

Les « Bonnes Femmes de Schorndorf », mosaïque en pierres naturelles de Gottfried von Stockhausen (1965) placée sur la façade nord de la mairie, rappelle le refus des citoyennes et citoyens de livrer la ville fortifiée de Schorndorf au général français Mélac, en 1688.

Das Burgschloss von 1538 ist die einstige Zitadelle der Stadtfestung Schorndorf.

Built in 1538, the castle was once the citadel of Schorndorf's fortifications.

Le château fortifié construit en 1538 était autrefois la citadelle des remparts de Schorndorf.

Natursteingewölbter Weinkeller unter dem Burgschloss

Vaulted natural stone wine cellar in the castle

Sous le château forteresse, cave à vin voûtée en pierres naturelles

Bei Führungen durch das Burgschloss erlebt man Geschichte hautnah.

A guided tour through the castle brings history to life.

Lors des visites guidées du château, l'histoire nous fait frémir.

Der Innenhof des Burgschlosses ist vom Fachwerk geprägt.

The castle's inner courtyard is characterised by half-timbering.

La cour intérieure du château et ses colombages

*Das Portal des einstigen
Spitals zum Heiligen Geist
mit den Wappen des Spitals (rechts)
und der Stadt (links)*

*The portal of the former
Hospital of the Holy Ghost,
with its (right) and the town's
coat of arms (left)*

*Le portail de l'ancien
Hôpital du Saint Esprit porte
ses armoiries (à droite) et celles
de la ville (à gauche).*

Das Pfründnerhaus des Spitals vom Archivplatz aus gesehen und die Wappentafel über dem südlichen Eingang (unten)

The hospital prebendary building, as seen from the Archivplatz, and coat of arms plaque above the southern entrance (below)

La maison des pensionnaires de l'hôpital, vue de l'Archivplatz, et les armoiries au-dessus de l'entrée sud (en bas)

Das Schorndorfer Stadtarchiv wurde in den Jahren 1785 bis 1788 erbaut.

The Schorndorf's archives were built between 1785 and 1788.

Les archives de la ville de Schorndorf ont été bâties de 1785 à 1788.

Im Stadtarchiv lagern wertvolle Bestände.

In the town archives valuable records are stored.

Les archives de la ville possèdent de précieux documents.

Fachwerkidylle in der Fußgängerzone

Idyllic half-timbered buildings in the pedestrian precinct

Les colombages créent une atmosphère idyllique dans la zone piétonne.

Einst war dieses Gebäude in der Johann-Philipp-Palm-Straße königliches Jagdschloss und Obervogtei; es wurde im Jahr 1555 erbaut.

Formerly this building in the Johann-Philipp-Palm-Straße was the royal hunting-lodge and high bailiff's office; it was built in the year 1555.

Construit en 1555, cet édifice dans la Johann-Philipp-Palm-Straße était autrefois pavillon de chasse royal et baillage principal.

Der Mondschein-Brunnen in der Daimlerstraße von Jürgen Goertz (1991)

Jürgen Goertz's "Moonlight Fountain" (1991), in the Daimlerstraße

Dans la Daimlerstraße, la « Fontaine au clair de lune » (1991) de Jürgen Goertz

Das Geschäftszentrum an der Kreuzung Schul-/Moserstraße

A shopping centre, where the Schulstraße and Moserstraße cross

Le Centre commercial au carrefour Schul-/Moserstraße

*Hübsch restaurierte
Fachwerkhäuser an der
Schlichtener Straße*

*Attractively renovated
half-timbered houses
along the Schlichtener Straße*

*Maisons à pans de bois
joliment restaurées
dans la Schlichtener Straße*

*Blick vom Kirchplatz auf
Fachwerkbauten im Winterkleid*

*View from Kirchplatz:
winter-clad half-timbered buildings*

*Vue de la place de l'Eglise
sur les maisons à pans de bois
dans leur habit d'hiver*

Fachwerk-Idyll in der Römmelgasse, links das »Haus auf der Mauer«, wo Schorndorfs Ehrenbürger Gottlob Kamm geboren wurde.

Idyllic townscape: half-timbered houses in the Römmelgasse; to the left—the "house on the wall", where Schorndorf's honorary citizen Gottlob Kamm was born.

Atmosphère idyllique des colombages de la Römmelgasse, avec à gauche la « Maison sur le Mur », qui vit naître le citoyen d'honneur de Schorndorf Gottlob Kamm.

Das Haus am Gumpbrunnen von 1685; der gusseiserne Brunnen ist der letzte seiner Art in Schorndorf.

The house at the Gumpbrunnen, built in 1685; this cast iron fountain is the very last of its kind in Schorndorf.

La maison du Gumpbrunnen date de 1685; cette fontaine est la dernière de cette manière de Schorndorf.

Die Weinstube »Sankt Urban« in der Römmelgasse

The wine-room "Saint Urban" in the Römmelgasse

Le bar à vins « Weinstube Sankt Urban » dans la Römmelgasse

Das »Daimler Carré« ist auf einem der ältesten Stadtquartiere neu entstanden; es beherbergt ein Hotel mit Restaurant, Läden und Wohnungen.

The "Daimler Carré" was newly built where once one of the oldest quarters of the town were situated; it accommodates a hotel with a restaurant, shops and flats.

Le « Daimler Carré » a été construit sur l'emplacement d'un des plus anciens quartiers de la ville. Il comprend un hôtel-restaurant, des magasins et des appartements.

*Kulinarisch und architektonisch
vom Feinsten:
das Hotel-Restaurant
im »Daimler Carré«*

*The very finest in cuisine
and architecture:
the hotel and its restaurant
in the "Daimler Carré"*

*Bel agencement architectural
et cuisine de gourmets:
l'hôtel-restaurant
du « Daimler Carré ».*

Seit 1861 ist Schorndorf ans Eisenbahnnetz angeschlossen. Der Bahnhof liegt unmittelbar am Marktplatz auf den Flächen der einstigen Festungsanlage.

Since 1861 Schorndorf has been on the railway line. The station lies directly on the market square, where the town's fortifications once stood.

Schorndorf est desservie par le train depuis 1861. La gare se trouve tout près de la place du Marché à l'ancien emplacement des remparts.

Die Bundesstraße 29 führt seit Juli 1997 kreuzungsfrei um Schorndorf herum. Blick von der Schornbachtalbrücke auf das nächtliche Schorndorf.

In July 1997 the major road B 29 was extended to include a circular by-pass around Schorndorf, a traffic system without crossroads. View from the Schornbach Valley bridge: Schorndorf by night

La B 29 contourne Schorndorf depuis juillet 1997 (sans feux). Schorndorf la nuit. Vue du pont enjambant le Schornbachtal.

Die Skulptur »Tor/Weg« von Gerda Bier auf dem Verkehrskreisel des Tuscaloosa-Platzes

The sculpture "Tor/Weg" by Gerda Bier, on the Tuscaloosa Square traffic roundabout

La sculpture « Tor/Weg » de Gerda Bier au centre du rond-point de la Place Tuscaloosa

Bummeln, einkaufen und einkehren in der Höllgasse.

Strolling, shopping and stopping for a drink or a meal in the Höllgasse

Flâner, faire des achats et se restaurer dans la Höllgasse.

Das Renaissance-Portal am »Alten Bad«

The Renaissance portal of the "Altes Bad"

Le portail Renaissance près du « Altes Bad »

Die Barbara-Künkelin-Halle ist seit dem Jahr 2000 das Kultur- und Veranstaltungszentrum Schorndorfs. Sie entstand genau 100 Jahre nach dem Vorgängerbau an gleicher Stelle.

The Barbara Künkelin Halls have been Schorndorf's cultural centre and festival hall since the year 2000. It was built upon the same site exactly one hundred years after the construction of its predecessor.

C'est au centre Barbara Künkelin qu'ont lieu, depuis 2000, les manifestations culturelles de Schorndorf. Il remplace un bâtiment qui avait tout juste cent ans.

Abendveranstaltung in der Barbara-Künkelin-Halle *An evening function at the Barbara Künkelin Halls* *Soirée-spectacle au centre Barbara Künkelin*

Im Hallenkomplex ist auch das Figurentheater Phönix untergebracht.

The hall complex also houses the Figurentheater Phoenix.

Le théâtre de marionnettes « Phönix » est installé dans le complexe culturel.

Die »Manufaktur« ist ein soziokulturelles Zentrum und Forum für Kunst, Kultur und Politik.

The sociocultural centre "Manufaktur" offers a forum for art, culture and politics.

La « Manufaktur » est un centre socioculturel et lieu d'expression artistique, culturelle et politique.

In der einstigen Eisenmöbelfabrik L. & C. Arnold befinden sich heute die Galerien für Kunst und Technik; links der Skulpturenhof der Kunstgalerie.

Today, in the former wrought-iron furniture factory L. & C. Arnold galleries of art and technology are to be found; to the left—the sculpture courtyard in the art gallery.

L'ancienne fabrique de meubles en fer forgé L.& C. Arnold abrite aujourd'hui les Galeries de l'art et de la technique. A gauche, la cour aux sculptures de la Galerie des Beaux-arts.

Der Ausstellungssaal der Kunstgalerie in der ehemaligen Schmiede der Eisenmöbelfabrik

The art gallery exhibition hall in the former forge of the wrought-iron furniture factory

La salle d'exposition de la Galerie des Beaux-arts dans l'ancienne forge de la fabrique de meubles en fer forgé

*Das Geburtshaus von
Gottlieb Daimler, Höllgasse 7*

*House number 7 in the Höllgasse
is where Gottlieb Daimler was born.*

*La maison natale
de Gottlieb Daimler se trouve
au numéro 7 de la Höllgasse.*

*Das Denkmal für den genialen
Erfinder an der Nordseite des
Rathauses.*

*Monument in memory of
the ingenious inventor on the
north side of the town hall*

*Le mémorial de l'inventeur de génie
en face de la façade nord
de la mairie*

Im Daimler-Geburtshaus ist ein Museum über Gottlieb Daimler, den berühmten Erfinder und Gründer der bekannten Motorengesellschaft, eingerichtet.

The house at which Gottlieb Daimler was born has been turned into a museum dedicated to the famous inventor, who was the founder of the Daimler Motor Company.

Un musée sur Gottlieb Daimler a été aménagé dans la maison natale de l'inventeur bien connu et le fondateur de la société de moteurs.

*Die Galerie für Technik in der einstigen Eisenmöbelfabrik widmet sich den technischen Entwicklungen im 20. Jahrhundert.
Im Bild eine kostbare Rarität der Luftfahrt-Geschichte: die Halberstadt CL IV (1918) des Flugpioniers Paul Strähle.*

The Gallery of Technology in the former wrought-iron furniture factory concentrates on technological developments of the 20th century. Depicted here, valuable exhibit—a real rarity in aviation history: the Halberstadt CL IV (1918) of the pioneer Paul Strähle.

La Galerie de la technique située dans l'ancienne fabrique de meubles en fer forgé est consacrée aux développements techniques du 20e siècle. Sur cette photo, une curiosité précieuse de l'histoire de l'aviation: le Halberstadt CL IV du pionnier de l'aviation Paul Strähle (1918).

Daimler-Motorkutsche aus dem Jahr 1886

The Daimler motor coach from the year 1886

Calèche à moteur de Daimler (1886)

Nachgestellte Szene zum »Red Flag Act«, einem Gesetz, das 1896 in England zur Sicherheit im Straßenverkehr erlassen wurde.

A scene depicting the "Red Flag Act", a traffic safety law that was passed in England in 1896.

Reconstitution sur le thème du « Red Flag act », une loi sur la sécurité routière votée en Angleterre en 1896.

Gigantische Dampfmaschine, Baujahr 1924, aus der Lederfabrik Breuninger in Schorndorf

Gigantic steam engine, built in 1924, from Breuninger Leather Works in Schorndorf

Gigantesque machine à vapeur construite en 1924 pour la tannerie Breuninger de Schorndorf.

Figürliche Darstellungen führen in die Arbeitswelt der Technikpioniere des Remstals ein: Gottlieb Daimler, Ernst Heinkel und Paul Strähle.

Life-like scenes offer an introduction to the working world of those pioneers of technology who lived in the Rems Valley: Gottlieb Daimler, Ernst Heinkel and Paul Strähle.

Des scènes reconstituées donnent une idée du monde des pionniers de la technique dans la vallée de la Rems Gottlieb Daimler, Ernst Heinkel et Paul Strähle.

Die neue, einladende »Arnold-Galerie«, in der Denkmalbauten und moderne Architektur miteinander verbunden sind.

The new, inviting "Arnold Gallery", in which old buildings and modern architecture are combined.

La nouvelle et séduisante Galerie Arnold, dans laquelle architecture moderne et bâtiments historiques sont imbriquées.

*Denkmalgeschützte Fassade
der Arnold'schen Fabrik
aus dem Jahr 1910*

*Listed for preservation,
the façade of Arnold Factory,
dating back to the year 1910*

*La façade de l'usine Arnold (1910)
est classée monument historique.*

*Nach dem Einkauf
geht's ins Straßencafé.*

*After shopping,
you can go to a street café.*

*Repos à la terrasse
d'un café après les emplettes*

Gasthausbrauerei »Kesselhaus«
 im Arnold

Brewery inn "Kesselhaus"
 in the Arnold

La brasserie « Kesselhaus »
 dans la Galerie Arnold

*Schorndorf von Osten
aus der Vogelperspektive*

*A bird's eye view
of Schorndorf, from the east*

Schorndorf vue du ciel, par l'est

*Die neue/alte Arnold-Galerie
von oben gesehen*

*The new/old Arnold Gallery,
as seen from above*

*Vue plongeante sur
la Galerie Arnold, un mélange
d'ancien et de moderne*

Gedenktafel für Daniel Steinbock, der durch eine Stiftung den Wiederaufbau der 1634 abgebrannten Lateinschule ermöglichte.

A commemorative plaque honouring Daniel Steinbock, who, through his donation, made it possible to rebuild the high school that was destroyed in a fire in 1634.

Plaque commémorative de Daniel Steinbock qui permit par une donation la reconstruction du collège de latin détruit par les flammes en 1634.

Das Stadtmuseum am Kirchplatz – links die einstige Deutsche Schule, rechts die frühere Lateinschule

The town museum on the Kirchplatz—to the left, the former state school and to the right, the former church school

Le Musée municipal sur la Kirchplatz; à gauche, l'ancien collège d'allemand et à droite l'ancien collège de latin

Die geologische und archäologische Abteilung des Stadtmuseums ist im ehemaligen, der herzoglichen Herrschaft vorbehaltenen Weinkeller der Lateinschule untergebracht.

The geological and archaeological section of the town museum is situated in the church school, in what was once the wine cellar which was only meant for the ruling dukes.

Les départements géologiques et archéologiques du Musée municipal sont installés dans les anciennes caves à vin du collège de latin, autrefois réservées aux ducs.

Stadtmuseum:
Produkte der Schorndorfer
Porzellanmanufaktur,
die von 1904 bis 1934 fertigte.

In the town museum:
items from the Schorndorf
porcelain manufactory, which was
in operation from 1904 to 1934.

Musée municipal:
productions de la manufacture
de porcelaine de Schorndorf
qui marcha de 1904 à 1934.

*Ein aus dem Jahr 1761
stammender Zinn-Pokal der
Schorndorfer Urbanszunft, die im
15. Jahrhundert gegründet wurde.*

*A pewter drinking-cup
from the year 1761, belonging to
the Schorndorf Urban Guild, which
was founded in the 15th century.*

*Coupe en étain de 1761
appartenant à la « Urbanszunft »,
une corporation de Schorndorf,
fondée au quinzième siècle*

*Tafelaufsatz der Schorndorfer
Handelszunft aus dem Jahr 1684*

*Centre-piece of Schorndorf's
commercial guild,
dating back to the year 1684*

*Surtout de table datant de l'année
1684 de la guilde des commerçants*

Die Weinberge des Schorndorfer Grafenbergs mit den romantischen Weinberghäuschen

Vineyards on the Schorndorf Grafenberg with their romantic, pretty little sheds

Les vignobles du Grafenberg, à Schorndorf, et leurs romantiques cabanons

Blick vom Weinbaugebiet Grafenberg auf Schorndorf. Im Hintergrund erstreckt sich der Schurwald.

View from the vineyards of Grafenberg down to Schorndorf. In the background the Schurwald can be seen.

La vue sur Schorndorf à partir des vignobles de Grafenberg. A l'arrière-plan, la Schurwald.

*Historischer Dampfzug
auf der Wieslauftalstrecke*

*Historical steam engine
on the Wieslauf Valley route*

*Train à vapeur historique sur
la ligne de la vallée de la Wieslauf*

*Das »Wiesel«, heute mit
modernem Dieseltriebwagen,
unterwegs im Wieslauftal*

*The "Wiesel", today a modern train
running on diesel, en route along
the Wieslauf Valley*

*La « Wiesel », aujourd'hui une rame
à moteur diesel moderne, circule
dans la vallée de la Wieslauf.*

Blick auf Haubersbronn
von Norden

A view of Haubersbronn
from the north

Le village d'Haubersbronn
vu du nord

Die Holzöfen in den Backhäusern der Stadtteile werden auch heute noch zum Backen von Salzkuchen und Brot genutzt.

Today the wood-burning ovens in the baking-houses in the town districts are still used for baking bread and savoury cakes.

Les fours à bois communaux dans les quartiers sont encore utilisés pour cuire le pain et les tartes salées.

*Der Kindergarten
im SOS Kinderdorf Oberberken*

*The nursery school
in the SOS children's village
Kinderdorf Oberberken*

*Le jardin d'enfants SOS Village
d'Enfants à Oberberken*

*Die evangelische Johanneskirche
in Oberberken von 1858*

*The Protestant church
in Oberberken built in 1858*

*L'église protestante de Oberberken
construite en 1858*

*Buhlbronn, der kleinste
Ortsteil Schorndorfs, bietet so
manchen idyllischen Winkel.*

*The smallest part of Schorndorf,
Buhlbronn, offers one
or the other idyllic spots.*

*Buhlbronn, la plus petite commune
de Schorndorf, présente
des coins très pittoresques.*

Kirche und Pfarrhaus in Schornbach,
besungen von Pfarrer Friedrich Glück (1793–1840)
im Lied »In einem kühlen Grunde ...«

The church and parsonage in Schornbach,
referred to by the parson Friedrich Glück (1793–1840)
in the song "In einem kühlen Grunde ..."

Eglise et presbytère qui furent chantés
par le pasteur Friedrich Glück (1793–1840)
dans la chanson populaire « In einem kühlen Grunde ... »

Die Feuerwehr in Schlichten
richtet auf traditionelle Weise
den Maibaum auf.

In Schlichten the fire brigade
erects the maypole
in the traditional way.

Les pompiers de Schlichten
dressent le traditionnel
Maibaum (Arbre de mai).

Die evangelische Pfarrkirche »Heiliges Kreuz« in Weiler, der größten zu Schorndorf gehörenden Ortschaft

The Protestant parish church of the Holy Cross in Weiler, the largest village belonging to Schorndorf

L'église paroissiale protestante »Heiliges Kreuz« de Weiler, la plus importante commune associée de Schorndorf

Die Kelter in Miedelsbach, Zeugnis bürgerschaftlicher Aktivitäten

The winepress in Miedelsbach, bears evidence of community activity.

La presse de Miedelsbach, témoin des initiatives citoyennes

Schorndorf

Eine Stadt, in der Geschichte erlebbar wird

Wer zum ersten Mal nach Schorndorf kommt, der wird erstaunt sein, dass sich nur wenige Schritte vom Schorndorfer Bahnhof entfernt ein geradezu riesiger Marktplatz öffnet. Er ist viel größer, als man ihn in einer Stadt erwartet, die ihre Stadtrechte bis in die Zeit um 1250 zurückführt. Damals befestigte und förderte der württembergische Graf Ulrich I. die Ansiedlung, die bereits in der Zeit der Staufer eine gewisse Bedeutung hatte. Mittendrin im Pflastergeviert steht das Rathaus von 1730, eingerahmt von stattlichen Fachwerkhäusern, die zumeist aus der zweiten Hälfte des 17. Jahrhunderts stammen. Ältere findet man nicht, denn 1634, mitten im Dreißigjährigen Krieg, wurde die württembergische Amts- und Festungsstadt von kaiserlichen Truppen in Brand geschossen. Außer dem spätgotischen Chor der nahe gelegenen Stadtkirche – nach den Stiftskirchen in Stuttgart und Tübingen die drittgrößte in Baden-Württemberg – und dem Burgschloss, ursprünglich Zitadelle der Stadtfestung, blieben nur wenige Gebäude erhalten. Und das in der damals für das Herzogtum Württemberg so bedeutenden Stadt. Um so bewundernswerter ist es, wie prachtvoll die wenigen Überlebenden ihre Stadt innerhalb der Festungsanlagen wieder aufgebaut haben.

Wer heute durch die Straßen, Gassen und über die Plätze schlendert, der erkennt am geschlossenen Stadtbild den einstigen Wohlstand, den eine zahlreiche Familien umfassende Oberschicht durch bauliche Ausschmückungen gerne zeigte. Diese bauliche Geschlossenheit wurde in all den Jahren von keiner falsch verstandenen Stadtsanierung aufgebrochen. Auf Schritt und Tritt wird Stadtgeschichte erlebbar. Schorndorf wurde bereits Mitte des 13. Jahrhunderts württembergisch und erlangte rasch eine besondere Bedeutung in wirtschaftlicher Hinsicht sowie als befestigte Stadt im Osten der Grafschaft, die ab 1495 zum Herzogtum aufstieg. Im 15. Jahrhundert war die Stadt ein beliebter Aufenthaltsort der Landesherren und wiederholt Tagungsort der Fürsten des Reichs. Einhergehend mit der Zunahme seiner landespolitischen Bedeutung, mit dem Sitz von Vogtei, Obervogtei und später dem Oberamt, entwickelte sich Schorndorf mit seinen bedeutenden Märkten auch zum anerkannten Zentrum für die Gemeinden der Umgebung.

Den Grundstock für den wachsenden Wohlstand in der Stadt bildete ab dem 15. bis Mitte des 18. Jahrhunderts der Weinbau im Remstal, allerdings mit weitaus mehr Anbaufläche als heute. Schorndorf wurde Zentrum des Weinhandels für das ganze mittlere Remstal. In dieser Zeit gab es allein in der Stadt sechs Keltern und heute noch legen riesige, mit Natursteinquadern gewölbte Keller Zeugnis ab von den enormen Lagerkapazitäten. Die gute Qualität des Remstalweins machte ihn zum Exportgut. Die Absatzgebiete lagen zum Teil in Oberschwaben, im südöstlichen Bayern und reichten bis ins Salzburgische, von wo die Fuhrwerke als Rückfracht Salz mit nach Schorndorf brachten. Dies war damals ein kostbares und teures Handelsgut, stellte es doch ein unentbehrliches Konservierungsmittel für viele Lebensmittel dar. Mit der Einführung des staatlichen Salzmonopols in Württemberg (1760) versiegte diese Erwerbsquelle, was einen wirtschaftlichen Niedergang der Stadt zur Folge hatte. Von diesem Rückschlag erholte sich Schorndorf erst um die Mitte des 19. Jahrhunderts mit der beginnenden Industrialisierung und der Eröffnung der Eisenbahnlinie (1861).

Obwohl Schorndorf nie die Privilegien einer freien Reichsstadt hatte, gilt es als sicher, dass die Bürgerschaft bereits im 14. Jahrhundert eine Schule einrichten ließ, denn im Jahr 1357 wird ein Schulmeister erwähnt. Die Lateinschule, unmittelbar südlich der Stadtkirche gelegen, brachte es zu großem Ansehen. Sie wurde auch unmittelbar nach dem Dreißigjährigen Krieg, dank der Stiftung eines ihrer früheren Schüler (Daniel Steinbock aus Schornbach), als eines der ersten Häuser wieder aufgebaut. Wichtige Persönlichkeiten erhielten in der Schorndorfer Lateinschule das Rüstzeug für ihre spätere Laufbahn: Jakob Degen, Professor in Tübingen; Karl Friedrich Reinhard, französischer Diplomat; Friedrich Heinrich August Weckherlin, württembergischer Finanzminister; Gottlieb Daimler; Reinhold Maier. Heute bildet das Gebäude zusammen mit der benachbarten, später entstandenen Deutschen Schule das Stadtmuseum, eine der größten stadtgeschichtlichen Sammlungen in der Region.

Den Aufstieg zu einer bedeutenden Stadt belegt auch die Gründung eines eigenständigen Spitals. Es entstand bereits Anfang des 15. Jahrhunderts und war im Jahr 1464 durch zahlreiche Stiftungen wohlhabender Bürger bereits so reich ausgestattet, dass es dem württembergischen Grafen Ulrich V. um 1464 in Fugger'scher Manier Geld verleihen konnte; allerdings gegen Übertragung aller Einkünfte aus dem benachbarten Dorf Weiler. Heute noch geben die stattlichen Gebäude des einstigen Spitals an der Ecke Archiv- und Palmstraße einen Eindruck von der damaligen Vierflügelanlage mit ihrem großzügigen Innenhof (heute begehrter Parkplatz).

Einer, der die Welt veränderte, wurde am 17. März 1834 in Schorndorf geboren: Gottlieb Daimler, der Erfinder des leichten, schnelllaufenden Benzinmotors und Gründer des Unternehmens, das heute als DaimlerChrysler weltweit hochwertige Autos produziert. Daimler hat sein Leben lang enge Beziehungen zu seiner Heimatstadt gepflegt. Sein Geburtshaus in der malerischen Höllgasse ist heute eine öffentlich zugängliche Gedenkstätte. Schorndorfs schönstes Fachwerkgebäude ist die Palm'sche Apotheke am Marktplatz; hier wurde

Johann Philipp Palm (1766–1806) geboren. Er hat, als Napoleon im Begriff war, ganz Europa unter seine Herrschaft zu bringen, als Buchhändler in Nürnberg eine Streitschrift verbreitet, die dessen Gewaltherrschaft anprangerte. Auf Befehl Napoleons wurde Palm 1806 in Braunau am Inn erschossen. An den Patrioten erinnert der Johann-Philipp-Palm-Preis für Meinungs- und Pressefreiheit, der alle zwei Jahre vergeben wird.

Dort, wo heute am Marktplatz eine seit Generationen im Familienbesitz geführte Konditorei mit Café zum Genießen einlädt, lebte einst Barbara Künkelin, Schorndorfs legendäre Stadtheldin. Sie hatte 1688, als der Magistrat der Stadt auf Anweisung der herzoglichen Regierung beschlossen hatte, die Festungsstadt den vor den Toren lagernden französischen Truppen zu übergeben, die »Schorndorfer Weiber« zum Widerstand aufgerufen. Erfolgreich, denn die Feinde zogen unverrichteter Dinge ab. An die »Künkelin« erinnert vieles in der Stadt, auch der Barbara-Künkelin-Preis, der alle zwei Jahre an Frauen oder Frauengruppen verliehen wird.

Noch manch anderen bedeutenden Persönlichkeiten kann man in Schorndorf auf die Spur kommen, wie der Malerin Ludovike Simanowiz (1759–1827), der wir ein berühmtes Portrait von Friedrich Schiller verdanken. Oder Karl Friedrich Reinhard (1761–1837), einem Schorndorfer Pfarrerssohn, der 1809 von Napoleon zum Baron de l'Empire, 1815 von Ludwig XVIII. zum Grafen und 1832 von Louis-Philippe zum Pair von Frankreich erhoben wurde.

Ohne den Schorndorfer Reinhold Maier (1889–1971) hätten sich die Badener und die Württemberger wohl kaum 1952 zum Land Baden-Württemberg zusammengefunden, das bis heute Deutschlands einziger gelungener Länderzusammenschluss geblieben ist. Der liberale Schorndorfer Politiker Maier wurde überdies erster Ministerpräsident des Landes.

Geschichte und Gegenwart sind in Schorndorf auf spannende Weise verflochten. Heimat- und Geschichtsbewusstsein werden gepflegt; gleichzeitig aber wird den neuzeitlichen Anforderungen der Stadtentwicklung Rechnung getragen – allerdings ohne die unersetzliche Vielfalt der überkommenen Stadtstruktur aufzugeben. Das macht Schorndorf so sehens- und erlebenswert. Der gewachsene Stadtkern, der ein Fotomotiv nach dem anderen liefert und auch schon Kulisse von Fernsehfilmen war, lässt sich bequem zu Fuß entdecken. Nicht umsonst ist Schorndorf eine Station an der Deutschen Fachwerkstraße. Einen neuen, anziehenden Kristallisationspunkt bilden die Geschäfte, Lokale und Galerien in der vormaligen Eisenmöbelfabrik L. & C. Arnold. Modern und großzügig fügt sich das Neue in die alte Stadt ein. Bummeln, einkaufen und einkehren, der Besuch von Kunstgalerien, Museen und die Begegnung mit Menschen macht Schorndorf zum immer wieder neuen und interessanten Erlebnis.

Schorndorf ist aber auch von einer geradezu lieblichen Landschaft umgeben. An den Südhängen des Remstals finden wir die Weinlagen des Grafenbergs. Auf der anderen Seite des Flusses liegt der Schurwald mit seinen ausgedehnten Forsten, den einst bevorzugten Jagdrevieren der württembergischen Fürsten. Hier liegen die Dörfer Oberberken und Schlichten, die seit der baden-württembergischen Kommunalreform in den 1970er-Jahren neben weiteren Ortschaften zu Schorndorf gehören. Im Nordwesten erstreckt sich die liebliche Hügellandschaft der Berglen mit ihren kleinparzellierten Wiesen, Feldern und den ausgedehnten Wäldern der Hochfläche. Eingestreut die Dörfchen Buhlbronn und Schornbach, letzteres in einer Richtung Schorndorf offenen Talmulde. Von Norden fließt der Rems das Flüsschen Wieslauf zu, an dem sich Haubersbronn mit seiner auf einem spätromanischem Vorgängerbau errichteten gotischen Wendelinskirche ausdehnt. Weiter nördlich bildet Miedelsbach den Abschluss des Stadtgebiets. Westlich im Remstal gelegen, präsentiert sich Weiler. Es ist mit Schorndorf eigentlich zusammengewachsen, besitzt aber trotzdem einen eigenen Bahnhof an der Remstalbahn. Von hier aus sind es dann nur noch 30 Kilometer bis zur Landeshauptstadt Stuttgart.

Winfried Kübler

Blumen-Haus in Haubersbronn

A flowery house in Haubersbronn

Maison fleurie à Haubersbronn

Schorndorf

A town, in which you can experience history

Anyone visiting Schorndorf for the first time is bound to be surprised, for just a stone's throw away from Schorndorf railway station lies an absolutely gigantic market square. It is much larger than would be expected for a town with a town charter that dates back to about 1250. At that time Count Ulrich I of Württemberg fortified and promoted the settlement, which had already held some significance in the days of the Staufer. Right in the middle of a cobbled square stands the town hall, dating back to 1730 and framed by stately half-timbered houses, which for the most part, were built during the second half of the 17th century. Buildings older than these are no longer to be found, for in 1634, in the middle of the Thirty Years' War, this Württemberg administrative fortified town was destroyed after coming under fire from the emperor's troops. Apart from the Late Gothic quire of the nearby municipal church—the third largest of its kind in Baden-Württemberg after the collegiate churches in Stuttgart and Tübingen—and the castle, originally the citadel of the town fortress, only very few buildings remained intact. A disaster of such enormity, in the very town that was, at the time, so important to the Duchy of Württemberg. It is all the more admirable then, how splendidly the few surviving inhabitants managed to rebuild the town within its fortifications.

Today, anyone who strolls through the streets, lanes or squares here, will recognise in the townscape—the architectural unity of which has not been disturbed by any unnecessary redevelopment—the former prosperity which the respectable upper classes, encompassing a great number of families, were keen to show in the architectural adornment of their town. On every corner, here, history is tangible. Schorndorf has belonged to Württemberg since the middle of the 13th century and has rapidly attained special significance—both in economical terms and as a fortified town in the eastern region of Württemberg County, which became a duchy after 1495. In the 15th century the town was popular amongst rulers and often served as a meeting place for princes of the Reich. Accompanied by the increased political importance of the town within the region—the administrative offices of various bailiffs and later, high bailiffs were situated here—Schorndorf, with its many big markets, also developed into a well-established community centre for the surrounding area.

From the 15th to the middle of the 18th century the basis for the town's growing prosperity was wine-growing in the Rems Valley, the extent of which was then far greater than it is today. At that time Schorndorf, alone, had six winepresses; today gigantic cellars, vaulted with ashlar blocks of natural stone, still bear witness to their great storage capacity. The fine quality of the Rems Valley wines made them suitable for export. Schorndorf became the centre of trade for the middle of the Rems Valley region. The wines were partly transported to Upper Swabia and south-east Bavaria, but also as far as the Salzburg area, from where the wagons returned loaded with salt. In those days salt was a precious and expensive commodity, indeed, it was indispensable for preserving all kinds of different foods. When, in 1760, Württemberg introduced its official salt monopoly, this source ran dry, resulting in the economical decline of the town. Schorndorf was only able to recover from this setback around the middle of the 19th century with the onset of industrialisation and the opening of the railway line (1861).

Although Schorndorf never possessed the privileges of a free old German Reich town, it is certain that the community had already established a school in the 14th century for, in the year 1357, there is mention of a schoolmaster. The church school, which is situated directly south of the municipal church, has gained respect and attention: It was one of the first buildings to be rebuilt immediately after the Thirty Years' War, thanks to a donation by one of its former pupils (Daniel Steinbock of Schornbach). Today, this building, and the neighbouring state school, which was constructed later, together accommodate the town museum. Here, one of the largest and most significant collections of local history in the whole region are to be found. At the Schorndorf church school various prominent personalities attained skills and qualifications for their later careers: Jakob Degen, who was a professor in Tübingen; Karl Friedrich Reinhard, a French diplomat; Friedrich Heinrich August Weckherlin, Württemberg's finance minister; Gottlieb Daimler; Reinhold Maier.

Schorndorf's development into an important town is also reflected in the establishment of a hospital as an independent body. It was founded in the 15th century. By the year 1464 it had gained so such wealth as a result of the numerous donations given by well-to-do citizens that, at the time, it was able to lend money to Count Ulrich V of Württemberg; however, this involved the transfer of the total revenue from the neighbouring village of Weiler. Even today the stately buildings of the former hospital on the corner of Archivstraße and Palmstraße still offer some impression of what the building with its four great wings and generous inner courtyard (now a busy car park) was once like.

One person who has changed the world was born in Schorndorf on 17th March 1834: Gottlieb Daimler, inventor of the light, fast-running petrol engine and founder of the concern that, today, under the name of DaimlerChrysler produces high quality cars world-wide. For the whole of his lifetime Daimler always maintained close contact to his home town. Today, the house at which he was born in the picturesque Höllgasse is a memorial open to the public. Schorndorf's most beautiful half-timbered building is the Palm's Apothecary on the market square. It was here that Johann Philipp Palm (1766–1806) was born. As a bookseller in Nürnberg he distributed a polemic pamphlet denouncing Napoleon's tyranny, just when the latter was about to gain control over the whole of Europe. Upon Napoleon's orders Palm was shot dead in Braunau am Inn in 1806. Every two years, in memory of this patriot, the Johann Philipp Palm Prize is awarded for freedom of speech and freedom of the press.

Standing invitingly on the market square, a confectioner's with its café, which for generations was owned and run by one family, is the place, where Schorndorf's legendary heroine Barbara Künkelin once lived. When in 1688, following the Duke's instructions, Schorndorf's magistrate decided to surrender the stronghold town to the French troops camped before its gates, she called upon the women of the town—the so-called "Schorndorfer Weiber"—to offer resistance. And it was a great success, for the enemy withdrew without having achieved anything. There is a lot in the town to remind us of Künkelin, including the Barbara Künkelin Prize, which is awarded to women or women's groups every two years.

Other important people can be traced back to Schorndorf, such as the painter Ludovike Simanowiz (1759–1827), to whom we owe a famous portrait of Friedrich Schiller; or Karl Friedrich Reinhard (1761–1837), son of a Schorndorf vicar, who was made Baron de l'Empire by Napoleon in 1809, a count by Ludwig XVIII in 1815 and then a French peer by Louis-Philippe in 1832.

Without Schorndorf's Reinhold Maier (1889–1971) Baden and Württemberg would most likely never have joined up in 1952 to form Baden-Württemberg, which, to this day, remains Germany's only successful federal state union and the first minister-president of which was the liberal Schorndorf politician, himself.

Past and present are interwoven in an exciting and interesting way in Schorndorf. Both a sense of the importance of what is native to the town and an awareness of history are upheld here and yet, modern demands of urban development are also taken into account—without, however, relinquishing the irreplaceable diversity of the town's traditional structure. It is this that makes Schorndorf so worth seeing and experiencing. The older centre of town, which offers many a motif for photographs and has also served as a backdrop for television

Frühling in Schorndorf Spring in Schorndorf *Printemps à Schorndorf*

productions, can easily be explored on foot. It is not just by chance then that Schorndorf is a stop along the German Framework Route. A new attractive focal point in the town are the shops, pubs, eating places and galleries in the former wrought-iron furniture factory L. & C. Arnold. Modern and spacious, the new blends in well with the old part of town. Strolling, shopping, going for a meal or just stopping for a drink, visiting art galleries or museums and meeting people, all these possibilities make Schorndorf an ever new and interesting experience.

The vineyards of the Grafenberg are situated on the southern slopes of the Rems Valley. On the other side of the river lies the Schurwald with its extensive forests, once favourite hunting-grounds of the princes of Württemberg. Here lie the villages of Oberberken and Schlichten that, among others, have belonged to Schorndorf since the Baden-Württemberg local government reform in the 1970s. Extending to the northwest lies the gentle, hilly landscape of Berglen with its small parcels of meadowland, fields and with extensive woods upon its uplands. It is sprinkled with the little villages of Buhlbronn and Schornbach, the latter of which is situated in a basin that opens out in the direction of Schorndorf. Haubersbronn, with its Gothic church Wendelinskirche that was erected upon the site of its Late Romanic predecessor, lies along the little stream Wieslauf that flows towards the Rems from the north; and further north still, Miedelsbach marks the end of the municipal area. Located in the Rems Valley and actually grown a part of Schorndorf and yet, possessing its own station along the Rems Valley railway line, Weiler points the way to the regional capital of Stuttgart, that lies a mere 30 kilometres to the west.

Winfried Kübler

Schorndorf

Une ville riche en histoire

Les visiteurs qui découvrent Schorndorf s'étonnent généralement devant l'immense place du Marché située tout près de la gare, une place beaucoup plus imposante qu'on ne s'y attendrait pour une ville qui a obtenu ses privilèges dès 1250. Ulrich 1er, Comte de Wurtemberg, fit fortifier et prospérer la cité dont la notoriété était déjà bien assise à l'époque de la dynastie impériale des Staufen. Construite en 1730 au centre de cette place rectangulaire, la mairie est encadrée par d'imposantes maisons à pans de bois datant pour la plupart de la seconde moitié du 17e siècle. Si on n'en trouve pas de plus anciennes, c'est qu'en 1634 – en pleine Guerre de Trente Ans – la ville administrative et fortifiée la plus importante du Duché de Wurtemberg fut incendiée par les troupes impériales. Peu de bâtiments en réchappèrent, mis à part le chœur gothique flamboyant de l'église toute proche, la plus importante du Bade-Wurtemberg après les collégiales de Stuttgart et de Tübingen, et la forteresse, ancienne citadelle du système de fortifications. Les rares survivants reconstruisirent de manière admirable la ville close.

De nos jours, le flâneur peut découvrir une ville qui, contrairement à bien d'autres, a été modernisée dans le respect de sa structure d'origine. On peut encore y trouver des traces de la prospérité d'antan au détour de chaque rue, chaque ruelle et chaque place, grâce aux nombreuses familles bourgeoises qui aimaient afficher leur aisance en contribuant à l'embellissement architectural de leur ville. Schorndorf fait partie du Wurtemberg depuis le milieu du 13e siècle. Elle connut un essor économique fulgurant, et son importance n'est pas étrangère à son statut de ville fortifiée du Comté de Wurtemberg et à sa promotion au rang de Duché en 1495. Au 15e siècle, elle représentait un lieu de villégiature très apprécié des seigneurs, et les grands de l'empire s'y réunissaient fréquemment. Devenue siège de la prévôté, et plus tard de la prévôté générale, Schorndorf connut un essor politique et, de surcroît, ses importants marchés en firent un pôle d'attraction pour les communes environnantes.

A l'origine de cette prospérité ininterrompue de la ville du 15e au 18e siècle, le vignoble de la Vallée de la Rems, qui couvrait alors une superficie bien plus considérable que maintenant. A cette époque, Schorndorf comptait à elle seule six pressoirs et, aujourd'hui encore, d'immenses caves voûtées témoignent des fabuleuses capacités de stockage de l'époque. La bonne qualité des vins de la Vallée de la Rems en faisait un produit de choix pour l'exportation. Schorndorf devint alors plaque tournante du commerce de la moyenne vallée. Le vin était vendu en Haute Souabe, dans le sud-est de la Bavière et jusque dans la région de Salzbourg, d'où les chariots ramenaient du sel vers Schorndorf. Ce sel était autrefois un bien précieux et fort onéreux car il représentait un moyen de conservation irremplaçable pour de nombreuses denrées. En 1760, cette source de revenus disparut suite à la création du monopole d'Etat au Wurtemberg, provoquant le déclin économique de la ville. Ce n'est qu'au milieu du 19e siècle que Schorndorf se releva de ce coup dur, grâce aux débuts de l'industrialisation et à la construction de la ligne de chemin de fer en 1861.

Bien que Schorndorf n'ait jamais bénéficié des privilèges d'une ville impériale libre, on sait que la bourgeoisie avait fait construire une école au 14e siècle puisqu'on a trouvé trace de l'existence d'un maître d'école en 1357. Le collège de latin situé côté sud de l'église principale de la ville jouissait d'une grande réputation. Grâce aux dons d'un de ses anciens élèves (Daniel Steinbock, de Schornbach), ce fut l'un des premiers édifices à être reconstruit immédiatement après la Guerre de Trente Ans. Ses locaux et ceux du collège d'allemand bâti plus tard abritent actuellement le Musée municipal. Sa collection consacrée à l'histoire de la ville compte parmi les plus riches et les plus importantes du genre dans la région. Au collège de latin de Schorndorf, des personnalités connues ont pu fourbir les armes de leur future carrière: Jakob Degen, professeur à Tübingen; Karl Friedrich Reinhard, diplomate au service de la France; Friedrich Heinrich August Weckherlin, Ministre des finances du Wurtemberg; Gottlieb Daimler et Reinhold Maier.

La construction d'un hôpital indépendant atteste également de l'importance acquise par Schorndorf. Construit au début du 15e siècle, il était déjà si riche grâce aux multiples dons des bourgeois aisés que, dès 1464, à la manière des Fugger, il prêta de l'argent au Comte de Wurtemberg, Ulrich V, moyennant la cession de toutes les recettes du village voisin de Weiler. Aujourd'hui encore, au coin de la Archivstraße et de la Palmstraße, les bâtiments imposants de l'ancien hôpital nous donnent un aperçu de l'ancien complexe, avec ses quatre ailes et sa vaste cour intérieure (parking fort recherché aujourd'hui).

Schorndorf a vu naître un personnage dont l'invention a changé la face du monde : Gottlieb Daimler, inventeur du moteur à essence léger et rapide, et fondateur d'une entreprise (aujourd'hui DaimlerChrysler) qui produit partout dans le monde des voitures de grande qualité. Tout au long de sa vie, Daimler a entretenu des relations étroites avec sa ville, et sa maison natale, dans la pittoresque Höllgasse, est aujourd'hui ouverte au public.

La plus belle maison à pans de bois de Schorndorf est située sur la place du Marché: c'est la pharmacie Palm, maison natale de Philipp Palm (1766–1806). Alors que Napoléon était en passe de soumettre toute l'Europe, ce libraire de Nuremberg a distribué un pamphlet dénonçant sa tyrannie, ce qui lui valut d'être fusillé à Braunau am Inn en 1806, sur ordre de l'empereur bafoué. Tous les deux ans, le prix Johann Philipp Palm, décerné pour la liberté de la presse et de l'expression, nous rappelle le courage de ce patriote.

Sur la place du marché, dans une maison abritant une pâtisserie – salon de thé appartenant depuis des générations à la même famille, a vécu Barbara Künkelin, héroïne légendaire de la ville de Schorndorf. En 1688, elle appela les « bonnes femmes de Schorndorf » à se révolter car, sur ordre du gouvernement ducal, le Conseil avait décidé de livrer la ville fortifiée aux troupes françaises qui campaient devant ses portes. La révolte avait été couronnée de succès puisque les ennemis furent obligés de lever le siège. La « Künkelin » est encore bien présente partout dans la ville, entre autres sous la forme du prix Barbara Künkelin, délivré tous les deux ans à des femmes ou à des associations de femmes.

A Schorndorf, on peut également trouver les traces de quelques autres personnalités célèbres. La femme peintre Ludovike Simanowiz, par exemple, (1759-1827) à qui nous devons un célèbre portrait de Friedrich Schiller; ou bien, Karl Friedrich Reinhard (1761-1837), fils d'un pasteur de Schorndorf qui fut élevé au rang de Baron de l'Empire par Napoléon, de Comte par Louis XVIII en 1815, et de Pair de France par Louis Philippe, en 1832.

Sans Reinhold Maier (1889-1971), lui aussi originaire de Schorndorf, les habitants du Bade et du Wurtemberg ne seraient sans doute pas réunis au sein du Bade-Wurtemberg (1952). Ce Land reste le seul exemple de fusion entre d'anciennes principautés qui ait fonctionné en République Fédérale d'Allemagne. Maier, homme politique et membre du Parti Libéral, en fut le Premier Ministre après sa création.

Auf Schorndorfer Streuobstwiesen

On natural meadows in Schorndorf

Arbres fruitiers de plein vent à Schorndorf

Schorndorf est une ville pleine d'attraits qui vaut le déplacement: présent et passé s'y mêlent de manière captivante. Tout en respectant le passé et en protégeant le patrimoine, il a été tenu compte de la nécessité d'urbaniser la ville, sans pour autant chambouler la diversité irremplaçable de l'ancienne structure urbaine. L'ensemble est très réussi et a déjà servi de décor à des téléfilms. Ce n'est donc pas un hasard si Schorndorf fait partie de la « Route allemande des colombages ». Le centre historique, qui s'est constitué au fil des siècles, offre des coins pittoresques à découvrir à pied.

Les magasins, cafés, restaurants et galeries d'art rassemblés dans l'ancienne fabrique de mobilier en fer forgé de L. & C. Arnold constituent un point d'attraction tourné vers la modernité. D'ailleurs, dans la vieille ville, moderne et ancien se fondent avantageusement et on ne s'y ennuie jamais: lèche-vitrine, achats, pause dans un café ou un restaurant, visite d'une galerie d'art ou d'un musée, rencontres ...

Les vignobles du Grafenberg se trouvent sur le versant sud de la vallée de la Rems. De l'autre côté de la rivière se trouve la Schurwald et ses grandes étendues de bois, autrefois réserve de chasse préférée des comtes du Wurtemberg. On y découvre les villages d'Oberberken et de Schlichten qui, tout comme plusieurs autres communes, sont rattachés à Schorndorf depuis la réforme communale du Bade-Wurtemberg dans les années 1970. Au nord-ouest s'étirent les grandes étendues de forêts des hauts plateaux et le doux paysage vallonné de Berglen, constitué de petites parcelles de prairies et de champs. Ici, le petit village de Buhlbronn, et là, Schornbach, dans une vallée allant vers Schorndorf. Venant du Nord, le petit ruisseau de la Wieslauf se jette dans la Rems, bordé par Haubersbronn et son église gothique St. Wendelin, édifiée sur des fondations de la fin de l'époque romane. Encore plus au nord, Miedelsbach constitue la limite septentrionale de la commune. Côté Vallée de la Rems, Weiler – bien que touchant à Schorndorf – possède encore sa propre gare pour se rendre à la capitale du Land, distante de 30 km : Stuttgart.

Winfried Kübler

Schorndorf im Winterkleid *Schorndorf, winter-clad* *Schorndorf enveloppée dans sa parure d'hiver*

Auf dem Einband:
Auf dem Schorndorfer Marktplatz

Einbandrückseite:
Herbstlicher Grafenberg

Vorderes Vorsatzblatt:
Schorndorfer Marktplatz-Panorama

Hinteres Vorsatzblatt:
Luftiger Blick auf Schorndorf

Cover photo:
On Schorndorf market square

Back cover:
Autumnal Grafenberg

Front inside cover:
A panorama of Schorndorf market square

Back inside cover:
Airy view of Schorndorf

Couverture:
La place du Marché de Schorndorf

Quatrième de couverture:
Le Grafenberg à l'automne

Page de garde avant:
Vue panoramique de la place du Marché de Schorndorf

Page de garde arrière:
Vue aérienne de Schorndorf

1. Auflage 2005

© 2005 by Silberburg-Verlag Titus Häussermann GmbH,
Schönbuchstraße 48, D-72074 Tübingen.
Alle Rechte vorbehalten.
Bildnachweis: Karl Senecky: Vorderer Vorsatz; Archiv Stadt Schorndorf:
S. 2, 13 links, S. 23 unten, S. 30 rechts, S. 37 links; Armin Kübler: S. 16, S. 17;
Blanz-Werbung: S. 44 unten, S. 45, S. 46 rechts; Zeitungsverlag Waiblingen:
S. 58; Stadtmuseum Schorndorf/Dr. Wolfgang Morlock: S. 62; Strähle Luftbild
Schorndorf: Hinterer Vorsatz. Alle anderen Fotos: Gabriel Habermann.
Übersetzung ins Englische: Hamida Aziz, Tübingen.
Übersetzung ins Französische: Claudine und Jürgen Bartelheimer, La Menitré.
Umschlaggestaltung: Anette Wenzel, Tübingen,
unter Verwendung von Fotografien von Gabriel Habermann.
Druck: Druckerei Grammlich, Pliezhausen.
Printed in Germany.

ISBN 3-87407-661-X

Besuchen Sie uns im Internet und
entdecken Sie die Vielfalt unseres Verlagsprogramms:
www.silberburg.de

Schwäbische Wirtschafts-Wunder
im Remstal und auf der Höh'

In hervorragenden Schwarzweißaufnahmen ist die Stimmung in 13 ungewöhnlichen Gaststätten zwischen Waiblingen und Schwäbisch Gmünd eingefangen. Renate Seibold-Völker und Michael Städele erzählen dazu die Geschichte der Lokale und deren liebenswerte Besonderheiten.

Mit einem Vorwort von Dietz-Werner Steck und einem Beitrag von Andreas Krohberger. Fotos von Gaby Schneider und Hardy Zürn. 96 Seiten, 130 Schwarzweißaufnahmen, fester Einband. ISBN 3-87407-387-4

Bertold Kamm · Wolfgang Mayer
Der Befreiungsminister
Gottlob Kamm und die Entnazifizierung in Württemberg-Baden

Die Entnazifizierung zählt zu den heikelsten Kapiteln deutscher Nachkriegsgeschichte. Dieses Buch rollt das Thema anhand der Biographie von Gottlob Kamm auf, der als Minister von 1946 bis 1948 für die Entnazifizierung im amerikanisch besetzten Württemberg-Baden verantwortlich war.

250 Seiten, 8 Abbildungen.
ISBN 3-87407-655-5

Hardy Zürn
Das Remstal

Seit vielen Jahren ist der Fotograf Hardy Zürn im Remstal unterwegs und hält in seinen Aufnahmen das Leben in den Ortschaften und Städten fest. Lorch und Plüderhausen, Urbach und Schorndorf, Winterbach und Remshalden, Weinstadt und Kernen, Fellbach und Waiblingen, Korb und Remseck – der Bildband gibt die vielfältigen Reize der Region exzellent wieder.

Text von Michael Städele. Deutsch – English – Français. 100 Seiten, 118 Farbaufnahmen, fester Einband. ISBN 3-87407-563-X

Dieter Buck
Ausflugsziel Remstal

30 genussvolle Wanderungen und Radtouren im Remstal und seinem Umland, vom Ursprung der Rems bis zu ihrer Mündung in den Neckar.

Wandern - Rad fahren - Entdecken. 168 Seiten, 102 Farbfotos und farbige Karten. ISBN 3-87407-512-5

Claudia Gollor-Knüdeler
Der Schwäbisch-Fränkische Wald

Dieser Bildband entführt in die Wälder zwischen dem Remstal, der Ostalb, Hohenlohe und dem Neckartal. Der Fotografin Claudia Gollor-Knüdeler ist es bestens gelungen, den besonderen Charakter dieser Landschaft einzufangen.

Text von Bernhard Drixler. Deutsch – English – Français. 100 Seiten, 104 Farbaufnahmen, fester Einband. ISBN 3-87407-535-4

Dieter Buck
Ausflugsziel Schwäbisch-Fränkischer Wald

22 Wanderungen und Radtouren zu den schönsten Stellen im Schwäbisch-Fränkischen Wald. Es geht durch kühle Wälder und Schluchten, vorbei an Mühlen und Wasserfällen, durch Weinberge und lebendige Städtchen.

Wandern - Rad fahren - Entdecken. 168 Seiten, 126 Farbfotos und farbige Karten. ISBN 3-87407-648-2

In Ihrer Buchhandlung.

Silberburg-Verlag